MAY WE NEVER FORGET
SEPTEMBER 11

The incredible photographic account of the hours, days, weeks and months following the horrific events of September 11, 2001.

presented by

The Journal News

www.thejournalnews.com

Copyright 2002 • ISBN: 1-932129-00-6

Published by Pediment Publishing, a division of The Pediment Group, Inc. www.pediment.com printed in Canada

CONTENTS

FOREWORD

Millions of words have been and will be written about the terror attacks of September 11, 2001, and the horror, courage and resolve that followed what The Journal News' next day headline called "A New Day of Infamy."

There were tragic, beautiful stories of heartbreak and heroism, loss and hope. But long after those words are forgotten, what will remain forever burned in our memories are the images captured by the photojournalists who covered the attacks, the rescue efforts and the numbing aftermath.

Among those journalists was the photography staff of The Journal News. On the morning of the attacks, the newspaper's staff mobilized within minutes of learning that the first commandeered jet had struck the World Trade Center. Editors, reporters and photographers rushed to the paper's newsroom in Harrison from their homes in New York, Connecticut and New Jersey. Many headed directly to lower Manhattan on instinct, even before the magnitude of the day's events was known.

Photographer Robert Sabo was sailing down the Hudson River on the Half Moon on an unrelated assignment and produced a memorable panoramic shot of the lower Manhattan skyline, smoke billowing from the doomed towers. Tom Nycz was on his way to Washington for another story and quickly changed course for the Pentagon.

Ten more photographers were dispatched to the site, but only two, Seth Harrison and Ricky Flores, were able to make their way to Ground Zero. Later that day, Flores photographed the unforgettable scene of three exhausted firefighters raising the American flag over the rubble of the collapsed towers. The others spread out over lower Manhattan.

In the months that followed, they and their colleagues - Stuart Bayer, Frank Becerra Jr., Matthew Brown, Peter Carr, Albert Conte, Amanda Davis, Vincent DiSalvio, Hai Do, Kathy Gardner, Morris J. Kennedy, Joe Larese, Larry Nylund, Danielle Perillat, Robert F. Rodriguez, Stephen Schmitt, Carmen Troesser, Mark Vergari and Carrie Yale - covered every aspect of the story. Free-lance photographer Susan Stava, Jay Capers of Gannett's Rochester newspaper and reporter Melissa Klein, who shot photographs as she was nearly buried beneath the debris of the first collapsing tower, also contributed to the coverage.

The photo staff spent countless hours with the firefighters, police officers, ironworkers and other rescuers who frantically searched for survivors at first, and then for remains when hope gave way to a grim determination to recover bodies. They walked with victims' loved ones as they scoured the streets, hospitals and shelters of lower Manhattan, snapshots in hand, determined to expend every effort to find their lost sons and daughters, mothers and fathers, spouses and friends.

They attended funerals, celebrating the lives of the victims and courage of their families while respecting their pain and privacy.

Their powerful collection of work is assembled in this book, "May We Never Forget September 11," in seven sections - Day One, Day Two, Day Three, The Missing, The Mourning, Patriotism and Recovery. Together, their photographs stand as a testament not just to the victims, their families and rescuers, but to the indomitable spirit of the United States of America, and her ongoing commitment to liberty and freedom.

DAY ONE

In the days that followed, September 11, 2001, would be remembered as one that began like any other late summer morning in New York. Children were returning to school, and New Yorkers were preparing to vote in a primary election. The lower Manhattan financial district came to life for Tuesday business as a gorgeous sun rose over the Manhattan skyline. But this day was not to be like any other. Unimaginable violence would unfold at 8:50 a.m. Eastern Daylight Time as a hijacked commercial jetliner crashed into the World Trade Center's North Tower. Two other commandeered planes would follow, tearing into the adjacent South Tower and the Pentagon in Washington, D.C., all as a nation watched in horror.

Photo by Carmen Troesser

▲ **September 11, 2001** began with a gorgeous sunrise over the Manhattan skyline.
Photo by Robert Sabo

◀ **The World** Trade Center's Twin Towers burn about 9:30 a.m. after they were struck by two hijacked commercial jetliners.
Photo by Melissa Klein

▶ **Smoke billows** from the World Trade Center's Twin Towers as thousands of employees inside try to escape the destruction.
Photo by Robert Sabo

■ **The destruction** could be seen from across the Hudson River in New Jersey as those outside the region watched in horror as the story unfolded on live television.
Photo by Robert Sabo

▲ **The South Tower** collapses at 10:09 a.m. *Photo by Melissa Klein*

◀ **People watch** in disbelief from a park in Jersey City, New Jersey, as smoke fills the New York City skyline after the collapse of the towers.
Photo by Frank Becerra Jr.

▶ **The North Tower** falls as a New York Waterway boat makes its way north on the Hudson River. *Photo by Robert A. Sabo*

▲ **In seconds** after the towers collapsed, a cloud of dust barreled north toward Park Row. Police yelled, "Run, Run!" People ran down side streets, the dust making it impossible to see and difficult to breathe. Many felt their way into office building lobbies and shops, where they gathered with other dust-covered people, gagging and gasping for air. *Photo by Melissa Klein*

▲ **Customers watch** news reports in the showroom of PC Richard and Son in Yonkers. *Photo by Matthew Brown*

▶ **Some people** on the street wear masks to protect themselves from the dust and debris left after the collapse of the towers. The North Tower collapsed at 10:30 a.m. *Photo by Melissa Klein*

▼ **Lower Manhattan,** as seen from Jersey City Heights, remained under a cloud of smoke for hours after the attack. *Photo by Vincent DiSalvio*

▲ **With no subway** or bus service, refugees from the World Trade Center and surrounding buildings make a slow trek north. Many gathered around cars with radios blaring and listened to news that the destruction had gone beyond New York City. *Photo by Melissa Klein*

◄ **Pedestrians evacuate Manhattan** by the Manahattan Bridge as smoke still billows from the disaster site. *Photo by Morris J. Kennedy*

▼ **A masked bicyclist** makes his way through streets filled with dust and debris in lower Manhattan, near what would come to be known as Ground Zero. *Photo by Seth Harrison*

■ **Firefighters hose down the Pentagon**, which was struck by a third commercial jetliner, American Airlines Flight 77. A section of the Pentagon collapsed at 10:16 a.m.
Photo by Tom Nycz

▲ **One of many helicopters** at the disaster site takes off in front of the visibly damaged Pentagon. *Photo by Tom Nycz*

▸ **Westchester County police officer** Stuart Smith stands ready as he guards the Kensico Dam, West Lake at Route 22 in North Castle. *Photo by Matthew Brown*

▾ **A distraught woman** makes a frantic phone call outside Grand Central Station. *Photo by Carmen Troesser*

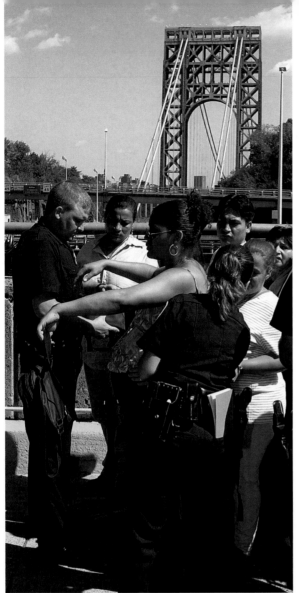

▲ ◄ ▼ **The George Washington Bridge** remained closed to vehicular and pedestrian traffic. By mid-afternoon, the Port Authority began using shuttles to get people across the Hudson River span. Several hundred people waited to board the shuttles, but everyone had to be searched. Members of the Bergen County Rapid Deployment Force supervised security around the shuttles. Many major roads, bridges and tunnels in the region were closed throughout the day.
Photos by Robert F. Rodriguez

◄ **U.S. Army**
Reservists stand guard with automatic weapons at the Army Reserve facility on Route 303 in Orangeburg. The military was on high alert following the terrorist attacks.
Photo by Vincent DiSalvio

▶ **Emergency**
workers barely could see a block in front of them as smoke and ash overtook lower Manhattan.
Photo by Seth Harrison

▼ **New York City**
firefighters are treated by medical personnel at Ground Zero.
Photo by Ricky Flores

▲ **Emergency workers** treat a colleague overcome by smoke while aiding in rescue efforts at Ground Zero. *Photo by Seth Harrison*

▲ **New York City firefighters** lift a fallen comrade killed in the collapse of the towers. *Photo by Ricky Flores*

◄ **Kevin Horan** of Staten Island reflects after escaping from the World Trade Center with minor injuries. *Photo by Seth Harrison*

▲ **New York City firefighters** remove rubble from where they believe they have found a fallen comrade at the World Trade Center in Manhattan. *Photo by Ricky Flores*

▶ **Firefighters** look up at the remains of the towers. *Photo by Ricky Flores*

◀ **Firefighters work** in the shadow of the shell of one of the towers after the attacks.
Photo by Seth Harrison

◀ **A firefighter** rests among the rubble.
Photo by Seth Harrison

▲ **A firefighter takes a break** on a demolished fire truck.   *Photo by Seth Harrison*

◄ **A New York** City firefighter sits on a fire engine at Ground Zero.
Photo by Ricky Flores

▶ **Firefighters** comb through rubble in the shadow of what would become the symbolic last remnant of the towers.
Photo by Ricky Flores

▲ **With both the Brooklyn and Manahattan bridges** closed to all but emergency vechicles, thousands of people walk across the Manahattan Bridge to evacuate lower Manahattan. *Photo by Morris J. Kennedy*

◄ **Martin Lyons** of West Haverstraw embraces his wife, Terri, who was waiting to pick him up at the White Plains train station after the attacks. Lyons had just arrived from Manhattan. *Photo by Matthew Brown*

▶ **Three New York City firefighters** raise the American flag from the rubble of the World Trade Center. *Photo by Ricky Flores*

▼ **Hundreds of people wait for hours** to donate blood at the Hudson Valley Blood Service in Elmsford. *Photo by Stuart Bayer*

DAY TWO

Thousands of emergency workers joined the rescue effort at Ground Zero, combing through the massive rubble in a frantic search for victims who had been buried alive. In a single day, the would-be rescuers removed 3,000 tons of debris. The official death toll remained at 82, many of them New York City firefighters. For families across the New York region with loved ones and friends missing after the attacks, hope remained alive as five survivors were pulled from the wreckage. The nation's military prepared to retaliate for what President Bush called "acts of war."

■ **Fire Department of New York fire engine 204** lies beneath a pile of rubble in front of the remains of the World Trade Center towers.

Photo by Stuart Bayer

▲ **Produce on a sidewalk stand** near the World Trade Center is covered with dust and ash as search and rescue efforts continue nearby. *Photo by Seth Harrison*

▸ **The NASDAQ building** shows a blank display at Times Square. The stock exchange was closed for nearly a week after the attacks. *Photo by Joe Larese*

▾ **Southbound traffic** on the Saw Mill River Parkway is diverted to exit at McLean Avenue in Yonkers after lanes to New York City were shut down. *Photo by Mark Vergari*

■ **Flowers were left** at the Brooklyn Heights Promenade for those killed in the tragedy.
Photo by Morris J. Kennedy

▲ **Emergency workers form a bucket brigade** as they move debris while searching for victims in the tangled mass of the towers' remains. *Photo by Stuart Bayer*

▲ **New York police officers** climb among the rubble as they search for survivors.
Photo by Seth Harrison

◄ **A New York City** Emergency Medical Services crew stands waiting for people needing medical attention.
Photo by Joe Larese

▼ **White Plains** Fire Department Lieutenant Rich Houlihan surveys the damage.
Photo by Stuart Bayer

▲ **Hundreds of firefighters** join the effort to remove debris in search of survivors they hoped had managed to survive. *Photo by Seth Harrison*

▲ **A New York City firefighter** takes a break from the search. *Photo by Joe Larese*

▸ **John Forbes of Denver** looks at photographic prints of the World Trade Center being sold as souvenirs by a street vendor outside Times Square. "It can definitely be a collector's item of sorts," he said. *Photo by Joe Larese*

▲ **A map showing the layout** of several levels of one of the towers remains standing as hundreds of recovery workers toil nearby. *Photo by Ricky Flores*

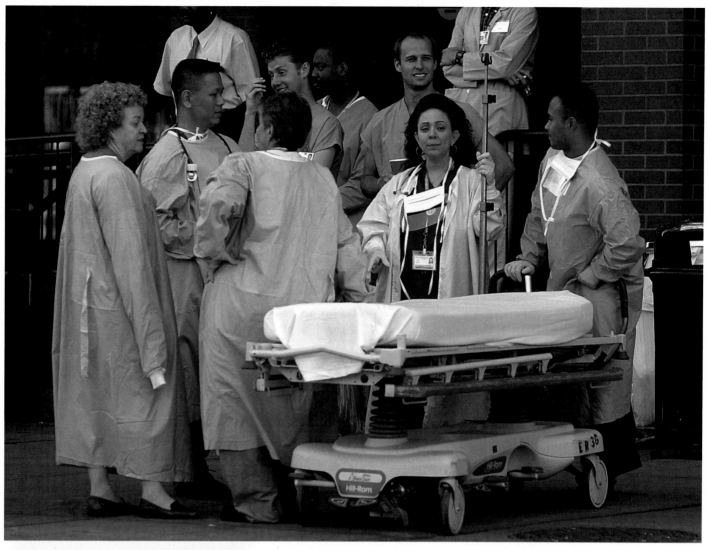

▲ **Medical personnel** wait on the street for victims, but very few would arrive. Several firefighters injured in rescue and recovery operations were brought in for treatment. *Photo by Robert F. Rodriguez*

▼ **Gordon Kappel, 3,** of Pelham, from left, and his brother, Shane Kappel, wait as their mother, Heidi Kappel, gives blood at Sound Shore Medical Center. Hundreds of people lined up to donate blood to help those injured in the attacks, and more than 2,000 pints were collected at the New Rochelle hospital. *Photo by Stephen Schmitt*

▲ **Suzette Lacher, 10,** a fifth-grader at Montessori School 27 in Yonkers, displays her journal entry for the day. The students were able to write or draw or both to express their feelings about the attacks. *Photo by Carmen Troesser*

DAY THREE

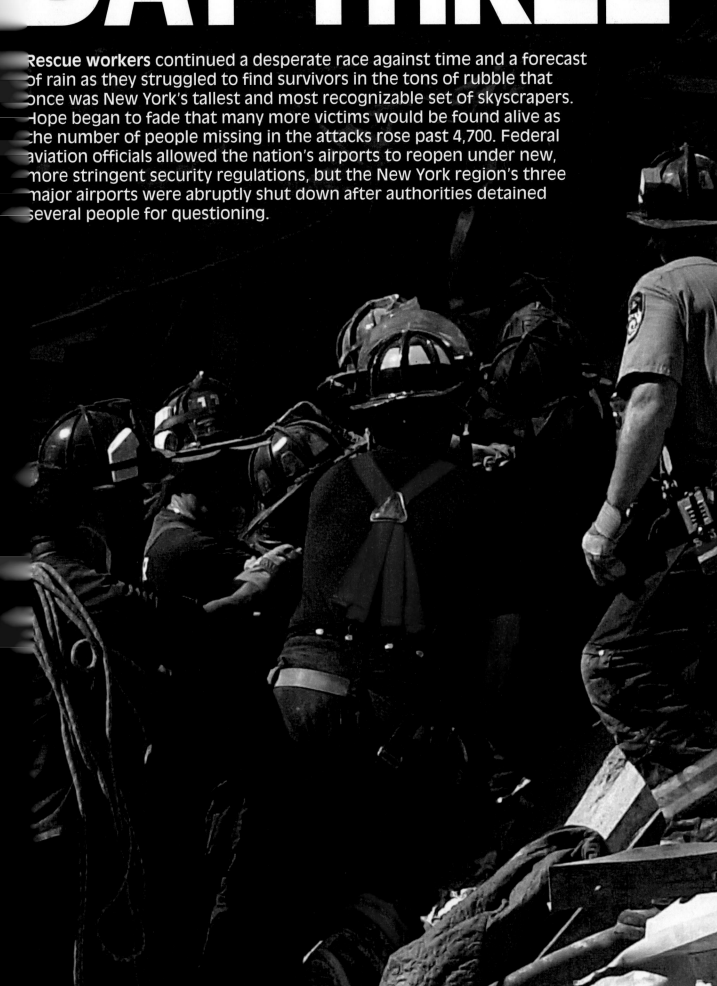

Rescue workers continued a desperate race against time and a forecast of rain as they struggled to find survivors in the tons of rubble that once was New York's tallest and most recognizable set of skyscrapers. Hope began to fade that many more victims would be found alive as the number of people missing in the attacks rose past 4,700. Federal aviation officials allowed the nation's airports to reopen under new, more stringent security regulations, but the New York region's three major airports were abruptly shut down after authorities detained several people for questioning.

■ **Rescuers carry a firefighter** from the rubble at Ground Zero.
Photo by Jay Capers

▲ **Broadway theaters,** including the Shubert and the St. James, dim their lights before the start of their shows. It was a symbolic tribute for those injured or killed in the attacks. *Photo by Matthew Brown*

▲ **Suffern High School students**
Jordan Steinberg, Bryan Goldstein, Mark Horton and Rich Reissman make peanut butter and jelly sandwiches to be delivered to rescue workers at Ground Zero. Students put together more than three-thousand sandwiches with supplies donated by Costco. Fred Greenberg, a school parent, organized the effort. *Photo by Kathy Gardner*

◀ **An unidentified protester** stands in Times Square as he holds a bible in the wake of the attacks.
Photo by Matthew Brown

▸ **Rescue workers** make their way through the twisted remains of the towers.
Photo by Stephen Schmitt

▾ **New York City** firefighters remove a body from the disaster site. *Photo by Stephen Schmitt*

▲ **Rescuers** look out from a pile of rubble. *Photo by Jay Capers*

◀ **Exhausted** fire-fighters grab a moment's sleep amid the rubble.
Photo by Ricky Flores

▶ **Jim Feldman** of West Nyack helps carry a donation of batteries and toothpaste to WFAS radio in Greenburgh. Feldman works at the station and had been unloading cars pulling up to the station all day.
Photo by Stephen Schmitt

▲ **Volunteer Parent Teacher Association** members Heidi Mele, left, and Judy Prieston of Hawthorne help close boxes of water and supplies donated at Westlake High School. The supplies were taken to firehouses in New York City.
Photo by Carmen Troesser

▲ **Brian Sargetz** of Manhattan sits at a makeshift memorial that sprung up at Union Square in New York City. Hundreds of people placed flowers, candles and left written thoughts and prayers to memorialize those killed and injured in the attacks. Sargetz, who works in lower Manhattan, saw the collapse of the towers and spent September 12 at the scene volunteering with the Red Cross.

Photo by Seth Harrison

▶ **Alison Cook,** left, and Lauren Alicandri set candles in front of the gazebo in honor of those lost at Ground Zero. They joined hundreds of others at an interfaith prayer service in Pearl River.

Photo by Susan Stava

◀ **A Rockland** Community College student holds a candle during a gathering at the college in support of the World Trade Center victims. *Photo by Peter Carr*

▼ **Bill and Lisa Rattner** listen to "Amazing Grace" at a prayer service in Pearl River. *Photo by Susan Stava*

THE MISSING

For days and weeks, relatives and friends of those lost in the attacks could be seen near the disaster site and around Manhattan. They brought pictures and posted fliers on makeshift billboards in the hope that someone, somewhere might be able to say their loved ones had been among the lucky few to have survived. Thousands would crowd the Lexington Avenue armory to register lost loved ones on a list that at its peak would include more than 6,000 names. Over time, hope would give way to grief, as the mission for crews at Ground Zero would turn from search and rescue to recovery and removal.

■ **Fliers seeking information** about people lost after the attacks filled a wall on Sixth Avenue in Manhattan. *Photo by Robert A. Sabo*

▸ **The sign outside** Christopher Blackwell's home expresses his family's hope he would return. Blackwell, a New York City emergency-medical technician, was lost in the attacks. *Photo by Joe Larese*

▾ **Trudy Calandrillo** of Brooklyn appeals to the media for "good or bad news" on the whereabouts of her brother, Joseph Calandrillo. She was among the group of victims' relatives gathered at the Lexington Avenue Armory seeking information about the fate of their loved ones. Joseph's remains later were recovered.

Photo by Robert F. Rodriguez.

◄ **Monsignor Dermot Brennan** holds four fingers up for the number of people missing from his parish as he gives his Homily at a Mass at St. Patrick's Church in Yorktown. Several priests, pastors and rabbis changed their sermons in the wake of the World Trade Center attack. Brennan told the congregation they should "seek justice, not revenge ... " in the 15-minute sermon to about 300 people in a packed standing-room-only church. *Photo by Matthew Brown*

▼ **Bulletin boards and shrines** like this one in Union Square, Manhattan, could be found throughout New York City. Thousands of images, shrines, paintings and candles were put up in memory of those lost in the attacks. *Photo by Ricky Flores*

▲ A bus stop on Sixth Avenue became a makeshift shrine as hope faded for hundreds of relatives of people missing at Ground Zero. Fliers seeking information about loved ones filled the bus-stop wall.
Photo by Robert A. Sabo

◄ A tearful Cathy Munoz of Queens holds a picture of her husband, Francisco Munoz, who worked at the World Trade Center, and their godson Michael. She was among hundreds of victims' relatives looking for their loved ones in the wake of the attacks. *Photo by Robert F. Rodriguez*

▶ Lorena Ocampo of New Jersey holds a sign with a photo of her best friend Fabian Soto, missing in the devastation at the World Trade Center. Ocampo stood outside the Armory at Lexington Avenue and 26th Street in Manhattan in hopes of hearing news about her friend.

Photo by Robert A. Sabo

▲ **Grace and Raymond Brengs** of Yorktown pray prior to the start of Mass at St. Patrick's Church in Yorktown. *Photo by Matthew Brown*

▾ **Jane Blackwell hugs her children,** Alexandra, 15, from left, Samantha, 11, and Ryan, 13, outside their Putnam Lake house as their father, Christopher Blackwell, remained missing. *Photo by Stephen Schmitt*

▲ **Erin Tappan** and Alicia Poster, 12, post a sign for family member John F. Plunket as Pat Cotton and Marianne Tappan wait. The family broke into teams and went from hospital to hospital searching for Plunket, who was missing in the devastation at the World Trade Center. *Photo by Robert A. Sabo*

▶ **Laila Shajahan, 4,** comforts her mother, Mansura, as they await word about their husband and father, Mohammad, who was among the missing. Friends and relatives gathered in the Shajahans' Spring Valley home as the family hoped against hope. Mohammad's remains later were found.

Photo by Kathy Gardner

◀ **A woman wipes away** tears during a candlelight march and vigil outside White Plains City Hall. The crowd took up four city blocks. *Photo by Frank Becerra Jr.*

▶ **Casey Cooney, 11,** whose father is a firefighter and was not injured, makes sure the memorial candles stay lit in front of the firehouse at West 48th Street and Eighth Avenue in New York. The firehouse had 15 firefighters missing after the World Trade Center catastrophe. *Photo by Mark Vergari*

THE MOURNING

Over time, thousands of families would accept the painful truth their loved ones had not survived the devastating events of September 11. Husbands lost wives, children lost fathers, and parents lost sons and daughters. The victims were newlyweds and first-time parents, single mothers and brothers, bond traders and receptionists, vice presidents and waiters. Some 343 were firefighters. In the end, the death toll was 2,823. Those who paid final respects and laid loved ones to rest knew they were not alone, that a nation grieved along with them.

■ **Nancy Shea** embraces her son, Peter, after a memorial service for her husband, Joseph Shea, and his brother, Daniel Shea, who were among those killed at the World Trade Center. The two men worked for Cantor Fitzgerald. *Photo by Carmen Troesser*

▲ **Cathy Schwarz** of Pelham breaks down in tears during a standing-room-only Mass at St. Patrick's Cathedral in Manhattan. Several thousand people crowded the cathedral on the National Day of Prayer and Remembrance.
Photo by Seth Harrison

▸ **Julie Simon** of New York City lights a candle before Mass at the service.   *Photo by Seth Harrison*

▾ **A New York City street scene** is reflected in the famous window displays at Saks Fifth Avenue, which were blackened in commemoration of the lives lost in the World Trade Center attacks. Only the words "With Sadness" were printed on the windows of the department store.   *Photo by Seth Harrison*

▲ **Harini Srinivasan** of Tarrytown lights a candle during a vigil at Patriots Park in Tarrytown. People came out to show their sympathy for the victims and their support for the rescue workers. *Photo by Tom Nycz*

◄ **Mary Huvane** of Sleepy Hollow lights candles during the candlelight vigil. *Photo by Tom Nycz*

▼ **Alicia Mulcahy** fights back tears as she holds her son, Liam, 2. More than 70 neighbors gathered at the end of Lark Street in Pearl River to participate in a candlelight vigil for the victims of the attacks. *Photo by Peter Carr*

▲ The tears flow from Spring Valley firefighter Lee Glick's eyes as chaplain John Kaprel gives a prayer for the fallen fire-fighters in the World Trade Center attack. The memorial for the fallen heroes was held in Memorial Park in Spring Valley.
Photo by Morris J. Kennedy

▶ The casket of Father Mychal F. Judge, chaplain of the Fire Department of New York, is led from the Church of St. Francis of Assisi following his funeral service. Judge per-ished while serving firefighters at the World Trade Center attack.
Photo by Robert F. Rodriguez

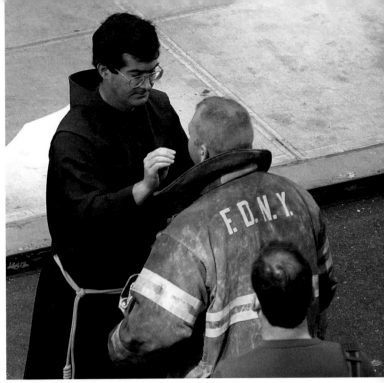

▲ **A Franciscan priest** serves communion to a New York City firefighter during the funeral of Father Mychal F. Judge. *Photo by Robert F. Rodriguez*

◄ **With a rosary** secured to his helmet, firefighter Steve Marley of Engine Company 48 in the Bronx attended the funeral of Father Mychal F. Judge. *Photo by Robert F. Rodriguez*

▼ **Then-New York Mayor** Rudolph Giuliani stands with his fire commissioner, Thomas Von Essen, and New York Lt. Gov. Mary Donohue as they pay their respects at the funeral of fire Captain Timothy Stackpoole during a Mass at the Good Shepherd Roman Catholic Church in Brooklyn. *Photo by Mark Vergari*

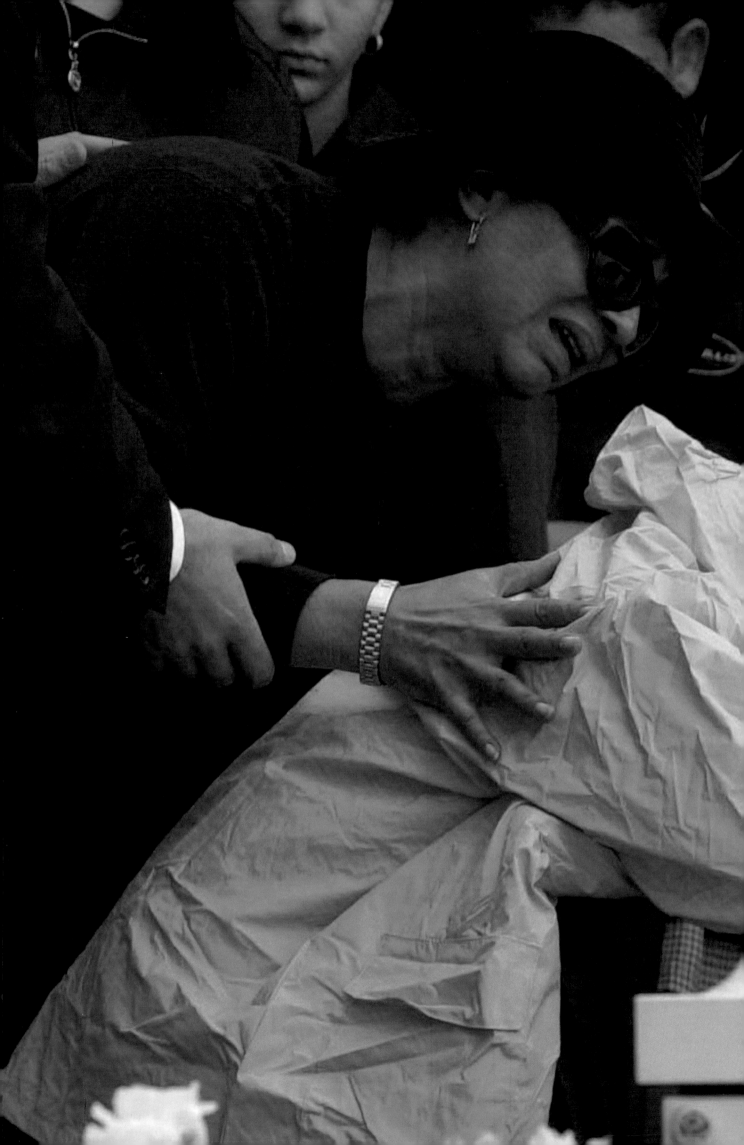

■ **Anna Jager** holds her grandson, 8-year-old Kevin Villa, as he cries over his mother's casket during her funeral at Mount Hope Cemetery in Yonkers. Yamel Jager Merino, an emergency medical technician with MetroCare Ambulance Corp., was killed at the World Trade Center while trying to rescue others. *Photo by Stephen Schmitt*

▲ **Emergency medical technicians** from MetroCare Ambulance Corp. and co-workers of Yamel Jager Merino hug outside the Sinatra Funeral Home in Yonkers after her service. *Photo by Stephen Schmitt*

▲ **Alison Crowther,** her husband, Jeff Crowther, and the Rev. Richard Gressle place Welles Crowther's ashes in the immurement wall in the memorial garden of Grace Episcopal Church. Welles Crowther, an Upper Nyack native who worked as an equities trader in Tower 2, died in the attacks. *Photo by Morris J. Kennedy*

◀ **Margaret Cruz** of Pomona, facing camera, hugs a friend after a memorial Mass for World Trade Center victim Patricia McAneny at St. Peter's Church in Haverstraw. In the background is a photo of McAneny, Cruz's partner. *Photo by Peter Carr*

▲ **Croton Harmon** and Edgemont soccer players participate in a moment of silence before the start of their game. Referee Ed Cassidy had called together both teams and asked them to take time to remember the victims of the attacks. *Photo by Matthew Brown*

▼ ▶ **West Point** cadets salute during a review in honor of lives lost in the attacks and a ceremony honoring the class of 1966. The '66 class lost more Army officers than any other graduating class of the academy.

Photo by Morris J. Kennedy

▲ **The New York Rangers** and New Jersey Devils line up on center ice for a moment of silence before the start of their September 19 game at Madison Square Garden.

Photo by Matthew Brown

New York City Fire Department Captain Mark Munelly of Hook and Ladder Company 2 holds a company helmet while a procession of firefighters enters St. Joan of Arc Church in Sloatsburg. A funeral was held for New York firefighter Dennis Germain of Sloatsburg, whose remains were found at Ground Zero.
Photo by Vincent DiSalvio

Honor Crowther attends a memorial for her brother, Welles, an equities trader killed in the attacks. Welles Crowther, also a volunteer firefighter, was later determined to be the hero carrying a red bandana who led other victims to safety in the towers before he died in the collapse. *Photo by Morris J. Kennedy*

Firefighters take the casket of Thomas Schoales into Immaculate Conception Church in Stony Point for his funeral. Schoales was with Engine 4 at the World Trade Center.

Photo by Kathy Gardner

Firefighters from as far away as Ontario, Canada, line the road as a procession for the memorial service of firefighter Daniel Harlin proceeds down Gleneida Avenue in Carmel. Harlin, of Kent, a member of FDNY Ladder Company 2, died in the attacks. The service was at St. James the Apostle Church in Carmel.
Photo by Joe Larese

▲ **Fellow firefighters** attend the funeral for Calixto "Charlie" Anaya of Engine 4, at Sacred Heart Church in Suffern. Anaya, a New York City firefighter, was lost while on duty at the World Trade Center. Anaya also was a volunteer firefighter for the hose company in Suffern.
Photo by Vincent DiSalvio

▸ **Jenna Jacobs** holds her 1-day-old son, Gabriel, who was born September 17 at Phelps Memorial Hospital in Sleepy Hollow. Gabriel's father, Ariel Jacobs, who was in the World Trade Center for a meeting, was lost in the attacks. *Photo by Stephen Schmitt*

PATRIOTISM

Out of the ashes grew a renewed sense of national pride. There were prayer services and candlelight vigils, impromptu gatherings where people would sing "God Bless America" and countless events organized to honor the victims and support the troops defending the nation. Young and old, Americans rallied around their flag.

■ **Wilfredo Mendez,** a bilingual pre-K student at Public School 13 in Yonkers, looks at a flag waving above him and his classmates during a school assembly where students displayed flags and sang patriotic songs. The students also heard speeches in many languages on what it means to be an American. *Photo by Carmen Troesser*

▶ **Anthony Gentile** and Samantha Shanahan, both 6, of New Rochelle, stand along Sun Haven Circle holding signs and collecting money for the New York Fire Department and the Red Cross. The children were selling soda, chips and homemade red, white and blue ribbons.
Photo by Stephen Schmitt

▾ **First-grade students** from the Pennington-Grimes Elementary School in Mount Vernon decorate paper bags with the American flag. The bags were filled with food and drinks for the rescue workers at the World Trade Center. All students and teachers in the school were making and filling bags – more than 400 in all. A note in each bag from the class read: "Dear Helpers, Here is a treat for you. Thank you for helping the hurt people and for cleaning New York City. Love Pennington-Grimes School." *Photo by Stephen Schmitt*

▲ **A large American flag** attached to one of the buildings at the World Financial Center flaps in th breeze as rescue efforts continue in the pile of rubble that once was the Twin Towers. *Photo by Mark Ver*

▲▶ **A gigantic American flag** is raised across the front of the New York Stock Exchange to prepare for the reopening of the building September 17.
Photo by Carmen Troesser

◀ **Rosa Mijares** of Yonkers wears the stars and strips as well as a World Trade Center memorial shirt. Mijares could not hold back tears during a candle and prayer vigil for the families and friends affected by the attacks outside the Yonkers Post Office. Her niece was at the World Trade Center that day and survived.
Photo by Stephen Schmitt

▲ **John Gauntt** holds up an American flag while riding the Staten Island Ferry into Manhattan on September 17. The ferry that day made its first trips to and from Manhattan since the attacks. Gauntt was bringing the flag to hang from his office.
Photo by Tom Nycz

◄ **Painters** Schaffer Carl of New Jersey, Alex Deveteri of Queens and Javier Estrada of Brooklyn paint a sign along the West Side Highway near 23rd Street in reaction to the devastation at the World Trade Center.
Photo by Robert A. Sabo

▲ **Joseph Green,** 4, of New York holds an American Flag at a memorial for the victims at Union Square Park. Joseph left a note at the memorial that said, "God Bless America."
Photo by Stephen Schmitt

◄ **Four-year-old** Brittany Zayas of Mount Vernon ties a red, white and blue ribbon to the fence in the Broad Street Playground. The memorial was started by the Fleetwood Neighborhood Association.
Photo by Stephen Schmitt

◄ **Nine-year-old** Russell Gewehr of Larchmont holds a homemade sign on Larchmont Avenue in Larchmont, yelling to cars as they pass "Honk If You Love America." Russell, his sister Haley and friend Anna Moser were having a roadside bake sale to raise money for the Red Cross. They hoped to raise $500.
Photo by Stephen Schmitt

▶ **Anne M. Dorner** Middle School sixth-grader Jilben Villanueva, 11, shows support for the nation during the Ossining school's Pride in America Day. Students made banners and prepared some 3,000 sandwiches for firefighters and rescue workers at Ground Zero. *Photo by Robert A. Sabo*

▲ **Blanca Males of Queens,** holds a candle while draped in an American flag as she stands with others at Canal and Church streets to witness the rescue efforts. Canal and Church was the entry point for all emergency personnel and the thousands of volunteers helping clear the rubble. *Photo by Matthew Brown*

▸ **Phillip Rivera** of Boston and Benicio Molina of Manhattan are wrapped in American flag beach towels, standing in Times Square as a symbolic tribute to those injured or killed in the wake of the attacks. *Photo by Matthew Brown*

▾ **Coming through** with red, white and blue are neighborhood kids on Frado Court in Stony Point who assisted Larry Sullivan, wearing an American flag bandana, a New York City police officer, in painting a 35-foot-by-25-foot American flag in the cul-de-sac. Wednesday, September 19 was Sullivan's first day off after the terrorist attacks. The paint, rollers and brushes were donated by Andrew's Paint in Haverstraw. *Photo by Vincent DiSalvio*

▲ **Lieutenant Brian Nee** of the Brewster Fire Department hangs a giant U.S. flag from the department's 100-foot ladder truck on Gleneida Avenue in Carmel before the start of a procession for Daniel Harlin. Harlin, of Kent, a member of FDNY Ladder Company 2, died at the World Trade Center. The service was at St. James the Apostle Church in Carmel. *Photo by Joe Larese*

◄ **New York Police Department officer** Sondra Duncanson marches into a fund-raiser for the children of Janet Alonso, who was killed in the attacks. The fund-raiser was at Terrace On The Hudson in Haverstraw. *Photo by Morris J. Kennedy*

■ **Lights shoot up over** lower Manhattan on March 11 as a memorial to the World Trade Center disaster. *Photo by Frank Becerra Jr.*

RECOVERY

The financial district returned to life as stock-market trading resumed six days after the attacks. Schools and theaters reopened, professional sports teams resumed play, and businesses in the financial district did their best to return to service. And, families tried to go on. For one month, two laser beams of light were shot into the New York City skyline as a temporary tribute to the Twin Towers and those lost in their collapse. In the end, just two of every five World Trade Center victims had been identified by the time the gruesome task of clearing the rubble and searching for remains was completed. A solemn, 20-minute ceremony marked the end of an effort that was to take a year but was finished in nine months.

▲ **Aiman Tubaileh** looks at the new New York City skyline from the Staten Island Ferry on his way to a meeting on Staten Island on September 17. *Photo by Tom Nycz*

▸ **Katie Castaldo** of Bayonne, New Jersey, and Arthur Crist of Roxbury, New Jersey, embrace as they look over the new skyline from Jersey City, New Jersey. *Photo by Mark Vergari*

▾ **Smoke from the fires** that burned for weeks after the attacks illuminates the smoky sky as workers at Ground Zero continue their search for remains. *Photo by Mark Vergari*

▲ **Smoke from a fire** still burning at 7 World Trade Center consumes the end of Greenwich Avenue in lower Manhattan. *Photo by Mark Vergari*

▲ **Mets Manager** Bobby Valentine helps to unload donations in the parking lot outside Shea Stadium. Many of the Mets' players and coaches aided the effort after their practice concluded. *Photo by Tom Nycz*

▲ **Emergency workers** with the Boone County, Missouri, Search and Rescue Team, walk toward the smoldering ruins as they prepare for another shift of rescue efforts.
Photo by Mark Vergari

◄ **Employees of the** Witkoff Group spray dust and debris off buildings on Nassau Street in the financial district in preparation to reopen for business September 17 along with the New York Stock Exchange and other businesses.
Photo by Carmen Troesser

▶ **Workers labor** to clean up dust and debris on Exchange Place in preparation for the reopening of the financial district.
Photo by Carmen Troesser

▲ **A departure terminal** at the Westchester County Airport indicates flights were about to resume after federal officials reopened air space. *Photo by Mark Vergari*

◄ **Religious items** such as this scapular were in high demand at James Dean and Family Religious Gifts in the White Plains Mall. *Photo by Stuart Bayer*

▼ **Soldiers stand guard** outside Ground Zero as part of Operation Noble Eagle. *Photo by Morris J. Kennedy*

◂**Jim** and Sujette Overstreet of Nashville, Tennessee, pause before a bronze statue of a fallen firefighter at Eighth Avenue and 44th Street in Manhattan. The statue, originally commissioned by the Firefighters Association of Missouri, was donated by the Missouri firefighters to the City of New York.

Photo by Seth Harrison

▲ **Workers on Wall Street** wear filtration masks as they walk past the front of the New York Stock Exchange. Wall Street and the stock exchange reopened September 17. *Photo by Mark Vergari*

◂ **A security guard** at the New York Stock Exchange checks the identification of employees as they wait in line to enter the building. *Photo by Mark Vergari*

▲ **Participants applaud** as police, fire and medical workers were on hand to ring the opening bell September 17 at the New York Stock Exchange.
Photo by Mark Vergari

▶ **People entering** the financial district wear filtration masks as they pass the bronze bull statue, adorned with American flags, on Broadway.
Photo by Mark Vergari

▲ **Traders on the floor** of the New York Stock Exchange greet each other as the exchange prepares to reopen. *Photo by Mark Vergari*

▶ **Emotions run high** as traders resume work. *Photo by Mark Vergari*

▲ **Cheryl Anderson** of New Jersey holds her bible as she waits in the long lines of people trying to get back to work in the Empire State Building. *Photo by Stephen Schmitt*

◀ **Television satellite trucks** park along West Street in lower Manhattan covering the disaster. Smoke from the site can be seen in the background. *Photo by Peter Carr*

▼ **New Rochelle firefighter** Raul Perez and his 10-year-old daughter, Elizabeth, collect money for the New York City firefighters' Widows and Orphans Fund outside Station No. 3 on North Avenue. The firefighters at Station No. 3 raised more than $6,000 in the first two hours of collection.
Photo by Stephen Schmitt

◀ **Elysia Schaller** leaves a message in front of Firehouse 14 for firefighters lost in the devastation at the World Trade Center.
Photo by Robert A. Sabo

▲ **Ten-year-old** Jodi Waizer gives her father, Harry Waizer, a hug during a visit to the Burke Rehabilitation Hospital in White Plains. Walking in behind her is sister Katie, 13. Harry Waizer was burned in the attacks. *Photo by Stephen Schmitt*

■ **The firehouse** of Engine 35, Ladder 14 and the 12th Battalion in Harlem lost three members in the World Trade Center attack of September 11.
Photos by Seth Harrison

▲ **New York City firefighter** Dennis Brosick of Engine 35 sits in the engine on the way to a fire call.

▸ **New York City firefighter** John Hunt adjusts the bunting hanging outside Engine 35, Ladder 14 and the 12th Battalion.

▾ **Firefighters from Engine 35,** Ladder 14 and the 12th Battalion have dinner together in the firehouse dining room.

◂ **Frank Silecchia,** a laborer with Local 731, hugs firefighter Brendan Ielpi of Ladder 157 on Christmas Day in the meal tent at Ground Zero. Ielpi lost his firefighter brother Jonathan in the attacks. *Photo by Mark Vergari*

▸ **Lynn McGuinn** hugs her daughter Carlie, 8, as the two wrap Christmas presents for cousins and other family members. McGuinn's husband, Frank, who worked for Cantor Fitzgerald, was killed in the attacks. Lynn decided to include a framed photograph of her husband with every Christmas gift to her family. *Photo by Seth Harrison*

▴ **K. Lee, 7,** of Manhattan volunteered to serve pumpkin pie to workers at Ground Zero. The Lee family delivered boxes of condiments to the Ground Zero food services location at South and John streets and then worked for the day to serve those working at Ground Zero. *Photo by Robert A. Sabo*

◂ **Cleanup continues**
January 2.
Photo by Stephen Schmitt

▾ **Small groups** of about 30 people at a time were led to a platform built by the City of New York for public viewing of the destruction. Thousands of people waited in line for the chance to view the site. *Photo by Stephen Schmitt*

▴ **Construction workers** wade through a flooded section of the pit where the World Trade Center previously stood. *Photo by Ricky Flores*

▸ **Family and friends** of victims who died at the World Trade Center in lower Manhattan look over into the pit on a platform set up by the Port Authority of New York and New Jersey. *Photo by Ricky Flores*

◀ Deputy Chief
Michael E. Collins of
the New York City
Police Department
walks away from
burned-out fire
trucks and emer-
gency vehicles piled
up at the Fresh Kills
Landfill on Staten Is-
land. All rubble from
the World Trade
Center was brought
to the landfill.
Photo by Seth Harrison

▲ **Employees'** identification cards from the
World Trade Center lie in alphabetized bins at
the Fresh Kills Landfill. *Photo by Seth Harrison*

◀ **A member** of the New York City Police Department examines a piece of paper as he and
another officer sift through rubble from the
World Trade Center at the Fresh Kills Landfill.
Officers examine every bit of rubble as it passes
on a conveyer belt. *Photo by Seth Harrison*

▲ **"The Sphere,"** an interim memorial to those lost in the attacks, is dedicated March 11 in Battery Park in New York City. *Photo by Stephen Schmitt*

◂ **Port Authority police officers** make their way toward a chaplain with the remains of a body recovered from the World Trade Center. *Photo by Ricky Flores*

▾ **U.S. Senators** Charles Schumer and Hillary Rodham Clinton, New Jersey Governor James McGreevey, U.S. Environmental Protection Agency leader Christine Todd Whitman and Cardinal John Egan are among those at a ceremony on the six-month anniversary of the attacks at Battery Park in Manhattan. A temporary memorial to the victims killed in the attacks was dedicated at the ceremony. *Photo by Seth Harrison*

⌃ Hundreds of thousands of daffodils planted after September 11 popped up all over New York City as part of the Daffodil Project. Here, daffodils in the shape of the World Trade Center make a flowery shadow in Brooklyn Heights.
Photo by Robert A. Sabo

▸ One of two Twin Towers beams remained standing May 27 as a symbol mourning those lost in the attacks. This one was cut down the next day and removed from Ground Zero two days later when recovery efforts ended.
Photo by Ricky Flores

■ **Construction workers** surround the last standing beam of the World Trade Center during a ceremony May 28. The beam was cut down and placed on a flatbed truck. *Photo by Carmen Troesser*

◂ **Former Mayor** Rudolph Giuliani consoles a relative of one of the victims of the attacks before the May 30 ceremony marking the end of the cleanup.
Photo by Seth Harrison

▲ A flatbed
truck carrying the
final steel girder
removed from the
wreckage leaves
the site during a
ceremony mark-
ing the end of the
cleanup.
Photo by Seth Harrison

▶ Members of
New York City's
emergency servic-
es carry a stretcher
containing only a
folded American
flag from the site.
Photo by Seth Harrison

Family members and fire-fighters salute as an ambulance containing a stretcher draped with an American flag makes its way up West Street to Canal Street, marking the official end of the recovery efforts.
Photo by Ricky Flores

▼ **An ambulance** containing a stretcher carrying only a folded American Flag leaves the site during the ceremony marking the end of the cleanup.
Photo by Seth Harrison

▲ **Tom McGowan** sits with his daughter Casey, 4, at their Basking Ridge, New Jersey, home with a photo of his wife, Stacey, who died in the attacks on the World Trade Center. Stacey, a former Grandview resident, was a senior trader at Sandler O'Neill. *Photo by Carmen Troesser*

▸ **Kevin Kittle** of Larchmont lost his wife, Helen, who was five months pregnant, in the attacks. The Kittles were married in April 2001. *Photo by Carmen Troesser*

▾ **Robert Alonso's wife,** Janet, was killed in the attack, leaving him to take care of his two children, Victoria, 2, and Robbie, 1, at their home in Stony Point.

Photo by Carmen Troesser

◄ **Alison Danahy**, 4, points to photos of her father, Patrick Danahy, on the way up the stairs to bed at her Yorktown home. Patrick Danahy, was killed in the attacks. Mary Danahy, the girls' mother, has posted photos of Patrick above their beds so Alison,4, Katie, 2, and Grace, 5 months, will see their father's image.

Photo by Carmen Troesser

▼ **Tom Cullinan** of Yonkers lost his wife, Joan Cullinan, an assistant at Cantor Fitzgerald, in the attacks. The Cullinans, who had been married for about a year, were in the process of hanging pictures and decorating their home.

Photo by Carmen Troesser

▲ **Following a reading** of the Declaration of Independence, Wolf-gang Lawton, right, of Mahopac watches as children sign a copy of the document during Fourth of July celebrations at Stony Point Battlefield. The reading was intended to remind participants of the courage and dedication to the cause of freedom that led soldiers and patriots to victory during the Revolutionary War.

Photo by Robert F. Rodriguez

▸ **Hasan Rasheed,** 9, helps paint a patriotic mural at the Yonkers Hudson Riverfest 2002 on July 4. *Photo by Seth Harrison*

▾ **Fireworks explode** before the Manhattan backdrop during the Macy's Fourth of July fireworks over the East River. *Photo by Mark Vergari*

▲ **The annual** fireworks off Manhattan took on special significance in the wake of the September 11 attacks. The event was dubbed "Macy's Fourth of July Fireworks Spectacular 2002: A Time for Heroes." *Photo by Mark Vergari*

◄ **Elizabeth Glynn** of Clinton, Connecticut, displays the spirit of America during the Town of Lewisboro's annual Fourth of July celebration at Onatru Farm. *Photo by Matthew Brown*

▲ **Fireworks light up** the lower Manhattan sky during the 2002 New York City Fourth of July celebration.
Photo by Frank Becerra Jr.